American History & Government

Native Americans in the Time of Lewis and Clark

by
Helen Sillett

Don Johnston Incorporated
Volo, Illinois

Edited by:

John Bergez
Start-to-Finish Core Content Series Editor, Pacifica, California

Gail Portnuff Venable, MS, CCC-SLP
Speech/Language Pathologist, San Francisco, California

Dorothy Tyack, MA
Learning Disabilities Specialist, San Francisco, California

Jerry Stemach, MS, CCC-SLP
Speech/Language Pathologist, Director of Content Development, Sonoma County, California

Graphics and Illustrations:

Photographs and illustrations are all created professionally
and modified to provide the best possible support for the
intended reader.
Pages 13, 22: National Archives and Records Administration
Pages 24, 32: Photo and copyright, Franz K Brown. Artifact prepared by Larry Belitz, Sioux Replications.
Page 47: CDC/ James Hicks
All other photos © Don Johnston Incorporated and its licensors.

Narration:

Professional actors and actresses read the text to build
excitement and to model research-based elements of fluency:
intonation, stress, prosody, phrase groupings and rate.
The rate has been set to maximize comprehension for the reader.

Published by:

Don Johnston Incorporated
26799 West Commerce Drive
Volo, IL 60073

800.999.4660 USA Canada
800.889.5242 Technical Support
www.donjohnston.com

International Standard Book Number
ISBN 1-4105-0440-9

Contents

Getting Started

In 1804, President Thomas Jefferson of the United States sent a small group of men on a long and dangerous journey. The group was called the Corps of Discovery. It was led by two young captains, Meriwether Lewis and William Clark.

Meriwether Lewis and William Clark

Lewis and Clark's job was to cross North America from one side to the other. They would be exploring a huge chunk of land. The United States had just bought this land from France. Nobody from the United States had ever made this journey before. Nobody knew for sure if it could be done.

But if anybody could do it, Lewis and Clark could. They were both strong young men who had served in the army. Clark had been an officer, and he was a good leader. Lewis was President Jefferson's assistant, and he knew about many subjects that would be useful on the journey. He had studied plants and animals, and he had read about medicine, too. Both men were ready for an adventure.

Lewis and Clark knew very little about this new land. But there were already Native Americans living on the land, and they knew it well. Hundreds of Native American tribes had lived all over North America for thousands of years. They spoke different languages, and they had their own ways of living. Sometimes they lived in peace with each other and sometimes they fought.

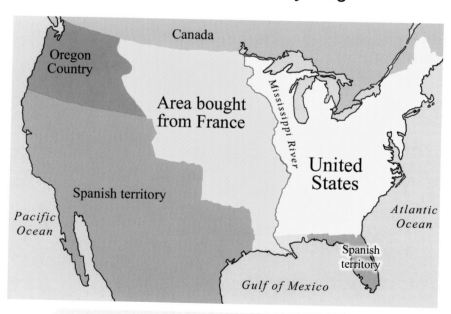

In 1804, the United States was much smaller than it is today.

What would happen when these Native American groups saw Lewis and Clark? Would they be friendly? Or would they attack the Corps? Nobody knew.

As it turned out, the meetings between Native Americans and the Corps of Discovery were very important for both sides. In this book you will learn about these meetings. You'll see Native American life through the eyes of Lewis and Clark. You'll find out how Native Americans helped the Corps of Discovery to complete its journey. You'll also learn how Lewis and Clark's journey changed the lives of Native Americans.

Article 1

Giving Gifts
and Smoking Pipes

Questions this article will answer:

• Why did Lewis get into trouble when he tried to speak the Shoshone language?

• How did Lewis and Clark show Native Americans that they wanted peace and friendship?

• Why did Lewis and Clark start to carry pipes?

In 1805, Lewis and Clark were in trouble. For more than a year they had been moving west. They had traveled along rivers until they came to the high Rocky Mountains. Now they had to find a way over the mountains before the winter snow came. They needed help badly, so Lewis took some of his men and set out to look for a Native American group that lived nearby. The group was called the Shoshone tribe.

Lewis and Clark wanted to get over the Rocky Mountains before winter arrived.

9

At last, Lewis and his men saw a Shoshone man on horseback. Lewis hoped that the man could help them. But what if he was dangerous? How could Lewis let the Shoshone man know that he didn't want trouble?

It is hard for people to communicate when they don't speak the same language. Put yourself in Lewis's shoes. What would you have done to show this man that you wanted peace and friendship?

Trying to Speak Shoshone

"Tab-ba-bone, tab-ba-bone." Lewis repeated these words over and over as he walked toward the man. Lewis was holding out some beads as a gift.

These Native American necklaces are made out of beads. Lewis and Clark gave beads as gifts to Native Americans.

How did Lewis know this word? He had learned it from a Native American woman who was traveling with the Corps of Discovery as a guide. Her name was Sacagawea.

Lewis had asked her to tell him the Shoshone word for white man. The Shoshone had no word for white man, so Sacagawea had given Lewis the word *tab-ba-bone,* which meant stranger.

"Tab-ba-bone," said Lewis again. Suddenly, the man turned and galloped off.

Why did the man leave? Perhaps he thought that Lewis was trying to start a fight. Lewis didn't realize that *tab-ba-bone* can also mean enemy.

As this story shows, sometimes talking isn't the best way to communicate — especially if the other person doesn't speak your language. Later, Lewis and Clark would learn other ways to show Native Americans that the Corps wanted peace and friendship.

Giving Gifts

Lewis and Clark knew that gifts were important to Native Americans, so the explorers had brought beads, clothes, mirrors, combs, rings, buttons, blankets, and knives to give away. They hoped to use these gifts to show that they wanted peace. Lewis and Clark also wanted Native Americans to see what kinds of things they could receive if they traded with the United States.

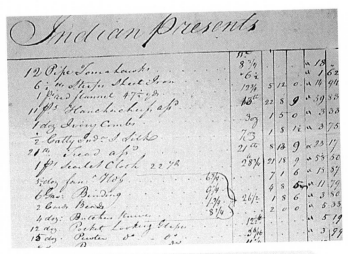

A list of presents that Lewis and Clark brought to give to Native Americans

Usually the gift-giving went well, but sometimes the gifts caused problems. Once Lewis and Clark met a tribe of Native Americans called the Teton Sioux. The leader of the tribe seemed to be a man named Black Buffalo, so the explorers gave him their best gifts. They gave him a red coat, a medal, and a hat. But the explorers didn't know that another man was struggling with Black Buffalo to become the leader of the group of Sioux.

This man seemed to be upset that the best gifts were not for *him*. He went over and pushed Clark.

Lewis and Clark brought coats and hats like these to give to Native Americans.

The other Sioux were standing along the bank of the river. They thought that a fight was beginning, so they pulled out their bows and arrows and got ready to shoot.

Luckily, Black Buffalo talked the jealous man out of starting a fight, and the men of the Corps went on their way.

15

Smoking Pipes

Along their journey, Lewis and Clark received many gifts from Native Americans — buffalo hides, clothing, feathers, and horses. But most often they received pipes for smoking tobacco.

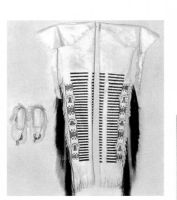

These are the kinds of gifts that were given to Lewis and Clark by Native Americans. President Jefferson put the gifts on display in his home.

Smoking pipes together was an important part of life for Native Americans.

Smoking pipes was a way to show friendship. Lewis and Clark were glad when Native Americans smoked pipes with them at the start of their meetings.

Lewis and Clark received many pipes as gifts from Native Americans.

During their journey, Lewis and Clark learned that smoking pipes together was a good way for them to communicate with Native Americans. Sometimes, the Corps gave gifts of tobacco to show that they wanted to smoke the pipe. They also started to carry their own pipes when they went to meet Native American leaders.

When Lewis first met a group of Shoshone, he pulled out his pipe right away and offered it to them. This was his way of showing them, without speaking, that he wanted to be friends.

Summary

In this article, you read about how Lewis and Clark communicated with Native Americans. Talking didn't always work, so the explorers used gifts to start friendships. Usually the gifts worked well, but once they almost led to a deadly fight. Lewis and Clark also learned to use the pipe to show Native Americans that they wanted friendship.

Article 2

Native Americans Help to Feed the Corps

Questions this article will answer:

• What new foods did the Corps of Discovery learn about from Native Americans?

• How did Native Americans make a food called pemmican?

• How did a tribe called the Clatsop help the Corps survive a cold, wet winter?

The Corps of Discovery traveled more than 8000 miles in two years, so of course the men couldn't bring all the food they needed for the whole trip. They had to hunt animals and gather plants along the way.

Lewis and Clark had to find their own food in places like this.

When hunting went well, the men had plenty of food, but at other times, they almost starved. In September 1805, the Corps camped near a creek.

Clark wrote in his journal, "I call it Hungry Creek, because at that place we had nothing to eat." At one point, just to stay alive, the men had to eat candles that were made of animal fat.

Luckily, the Corps received help from many Native American tribes. In this article, you'll read how Native Americans helped the Corps to get food. The men might have starved to death without this help.

Bread and Breadroot

Native Americans were experts at getting what they needed from the land around them. They showed Lewis and Clark roots and plants that they could eat.

One day, Clark and a few of the men went ahead of the rest of the Corps, and they met a tribe called the Nez Perce. The Nez Perce gave Clark some bread that was made from a vegetable called camas root.

This photo of a Nez Perce chief was taken about 70 years after Lewis and Clark's journey.

Clark and his men liked the bread, but later that night, they became sick with gas and the runs. A few days later, the rest of the Corps showed up. Clark warned the Corps about the camas root bread, but the men were hungry, so they ate it anyway.

Lewis loved the bread and ate a lot of it. That night, the men became ill, and Lewis was hit the hardest.

The men also learned about new foods from Sacagawea, the Native American woman who joined the Corps for part of the journey. She taught them how her tribe used a vegetable called breadroot. Sometimes they ate the breadroot raw. At other times, they dried it out and pounded it into a powder. They put the powder into soups to make the soups thicker.

Sacagawea joined the Corps for part of the journey.

Pemmican

Some Native American tribes made a food called **pemmican**. They made the pemmican out of meat, berries, and fat. First, they cut the meat into thin strips and laid the strips out to dry, like beef jerky. Then they pounded the dried meat into a powder. After this, they mixed the powder with berries and hot melted fat. Next, they made the mixture into flat cakes. The last step was to lay the flat cakes out to dry until they were hard.

Photo and copyright, Franz K Brown. Artifact prepared by Larry Belitz, Sioux Replications.

Flat cakes of pemmican

At first, the Corps got pemmican from the Teton Sioux and from a tribe called the Mandans. But later on, the men made their own pemmican. It was a great food to take on a journey because it was easy to carry and it lasted for a long time without rotting. Pemmican was the perfect food to eat when there was no time to cook, and when there was no fresh meat.

A Hard Winter

The men crossed the Rocky Mountains in late 1805. After they crossed the mountains, they spent a cold, wet winter near the Pacific Ocean.

The men spent a cold, wet winter near the Pacific Ocean.

Winter in the wilderness can be very dangerous, especially if you don't know where to find food. Luckily, a tribe called the Clatsop helped the Corps survive the winter. The Clatsop told the Corps where to hunt elk. They also sold the Corps a useful root called wappato, which the men cooked and ate with meat, like a potato.

The men of the Corps built a wooden fort for shelter during the winter. This is what the fort looked like.

One day the Clatsop told the Corps about a whale that had washed up on a nearby beach. Some of the men of the Corps rushed to the beach to get meat and **blubber** (fat) from the whale.

Sacagawea went with them. But when they got to the beach, they found that another tribe had already cut all the meat and blubber off the whale.

Summary

In this article, you learned how Native Americans helped the Corps of Discovery get food to survive on their long journey. The men learned about new vegetables and roots from Native Americans. They learned how to make a useful food called pemmican. During a cold winter near the Pacific Ocean, a tribe called the Clatsop helped the Corps survive. The Corps ended up trading with this tribe for blubber to eat. The blubber helped them get through the winter.

Article 3

Native American Houses

Questions this article will answer:

- Why did some Native American tribes live in shelters called tipis?

- What kind of house was built by the Mandan tribe?

- Why did Native Americans build two different kinds of houses along the Columbia River?

A house with a steep, slanted roof

Take a look at the roof on this house. Why do you think it was built with a steep, slanted roof? Here's a hint. It often snows where this house was built. If the roof was flat, what do you think might happen after a big snowstorm?

The roof on this house is perfect for a place that gets a lot of snow. If it was flat, snow would pile up on top and the roof might cave in.

29

As this example shows, a house needs to fit the place where it is built. On their journey west, Lewis and Clark saw many different kinds of Native American houses. They found that each group built shelters that fit the places where they lived.

Tipis on the Great Plains

Lewis and Clark left the town of St. Louis in the spring of 1804. They traveled along the Missouri River through the Great Plains.

The Corps of Discovery traveled along the Missouri River through the Great Plains.

This was a huge area of grassy land. There they entered the **territory** (area) of a tribe called the Yankton Sioux.

The Yankton were one of the **nomadic** tribes of the Great Plains. Nomadic people are people who move around from place to place. The Yankton traveled in small groups on horseback. They moved around to follow the giant herds of buffalo that wandered across the plains. The tribe hunted buffalo for food and other needs.

Lewis and Clark wanted to meet with the Yankton, so they sent a man ahead to look for the tribe. When he got back, the man told them about seeing the Yanktons' shelters. He said the shelters were made of buffalo skins that were painted different colors.

Nobody in the Corps of Discovery had seen this kind of shelter before.

The man was talking about **tipis**, which were made with buffalo skins and wooden poles. Tipis were perfect for the nomads who followed the buffalo because a tipi could be set up and taken down in about 15 minutes. This made it easy for the Yankton to move and take their houses with them.

Photo and copyright, Franz K Brown. Artifact prepared by Larry Belitz, Sioux Replications.

Tribes that moved around a lot needed homes that they could take with them, like this tipi.

Villages on the Plains

The Corps spent one cold winter on the Great Plains near a tribe called the Mandans. The Mandans did not move around like the Yankton. The Mandans stayed in one place because they were an **agricultural** tribe. This means that they farmed the land and grew food like corn, beans, and pumpkins. The Mandans needed their homes to last a long time, so they built **lodges** instead of tipis. The lodges were made out of wooden posts and dirt.

This is what a Mandan lodge looked like.

Each village had hundreds of lodges, and each lodge was big enough to hold several families and their horses. The Mandans and another group, the Hidatsas, lived in five villages. There were 4500 people living in these villages — more people than there were in the city of Washington, D.C., at that time.

Shelters Along the Columbia River

The last part of Lewis and Clark's journey to the Pacific coast was along the Columbia River. The Cascade Mountains divide this area into an eastern part and a western part. Each part has different weather. The western side is very wet, and the eastern side is very dry. The western side of the mountains is covered with thick rainforests, and it gets five feet of rain a year.

The eastern side of the mountains is open country where there are not so many trees, and it gets less than ten inches of rain each year.

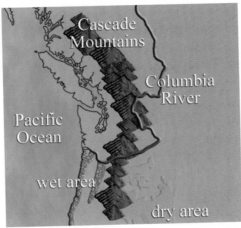

This map shows the wet area on the western side of the Cascade Mountains and the dry area on the eastern side of the mountains.

As they crossed the Cascade Mountains, Lewis and Clark noticed that there were two very different kinds of houses on the eastern and western sides of the mountains. See if you can guess which kind of weather these houses were built for. One kind of house was known as a "mat lodge."

It was made out of grasses and reeds that were woven into mats. The roofs on the mat lodges were flat. The other kind of house was made out of thick wooden boards. The roofs were slanted, and they were sometimes covered with two layers of wood.

If you guessed that the wooden house belonged in the rainy weather, you're right. Houses in a rainy place need a thick, slanted roof to carry the rainwater away. The mat lodges with their flat roofs were perfect shelters for dry weather.

Summary

In this article, you read about some of the Native American shelters that Lewis and Clark saw on their journey. Nomads on the Great Plains lived in tipis, while agricultural tribes like the Mandans built lodges out of dirt. The two kinds of houses along the Columbia River fit the different kinds of weather on the eastern and western sides of the mountains.

Article 4

The Useful Buffalo

Questions this article will answer:

- **How did some Native Americans use buffalo skins to make tipis?**

- **How did the Mandans use buffalo skins to make boats?**

During Lewis and Clark's winter on the Great Plains, the Mandans invited the men to join them on a buffalo hunt. On the night before the hunt, Mandan warriors put on robes made from the heads and skins of buffalo. Then they danced around a fire and stomped their feet. This dance was called a buffalo-calling. The Mandans believed that the buffalo-calling dance would bring them good luck on their hunt.

It was important for the men to have a good hunt because the Mandans used the buffalo for everything — meat, clothes, blankets, boats, ropes, and farming tools. The nomadic tribes on the plains also depended on the buffalo for their way of life. In this article, you'll look at two of the ways that Native Americans used buffalo skins.

Many Native Americans depended on the buffalo for their way of life.

Making a Tipi

Nomadic tribes like the Teton Sioux used buffalo **hides** (skins) to make tipis. Women were the ones who did this job, and they worked together in groups.

The first step in making a tipi was to prepare the buffalo hide. After the hides were cut from the dead buffalo, the Sioux scraped the hides to remove all the hair.

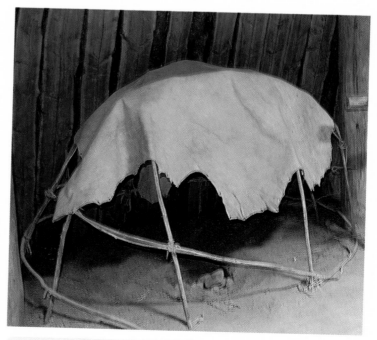

The hide of a buffalo, with all the hair scraped off

Next, the hides had to be **tanned**. Tanning means treating the hide so that it will last for a long time. The women tanned the hides with buffalo brains. One brain was used for each hide. The women boiled the brains in water for about 15 minutes. Then they rubbed the brains into the hides and poured the water all over the skins.

After the hides were tanned, they had to be stretched until they were smooth. Then they needed to be smoked. To smoke the hides, the women hung them near a fire. The smoke made the hides last longer.

Finally, the women sewed the hides together so that they could be hung over the poles of the tipi. A tipi was about 14 feet tall and weighed about 95 pounds. A well-tanned tipi would last for about ten years.

A tipi made from buffalo hides

Making a Boat

Imagine that you are stuck in the wilderness near a river and you are looking for a way to get out. All you have with you is a buffalo skin and some branches.

Can you think of a way to use these things to get yourself out of the wilderness?

Four members of the Corps of Discovery faced this problem. Captain Clark had sent these men to take some horses to the Mandans. On the way, another group of Native Americans stole the horses. The men were miles away from the rest of the Corps. They knew they would never be able to catch up with the other men on foot.

Luckily, the men had seen the Mandans make sturdy boats out of a buffalo hide and branches. The boats were called **bull boats**. To make the boats, the Mandans tied two branches together to make a circle.

This circle was the top of the boat. Then they used more branches to make a frame that was shaped like a bowl. Finally, they stretched a buffalo hide over the frame and they tied it to the wood.

A bull boat

The bull boats were strong, and they didn't tip over, even when the river was choppy and rough. After making their own bull boats, Clark's men were able to travel along a river until they caught up with Clark 12 days later.

Summary

In this article, you read about two ways that buffalo hides were used. Native Americans on the Great Plains used the hides to make tipis. The Mandans made bull boats out of buffalo hides and branches. Some of Lewis and Clark's men had to build their own bull boats to get themselves out of the wilderness.

Article 5

Changes on the Great Plains

Questions this article will answer:

• **What disease killed many Native Americans on the Great Plains?**

• **What happened to Native Americans after white settlers began moving to the Great Plains?**

In August 1804, Lewis and Clark were surprised to come across a Native American village that had been burned to the ground. Two months later they found some villages of the Arikara tribe. They had expected to find many people in these villages, but the villages were empty.

The empty villages were a sign of the changes that were starting to happen on the Great Plains. In this article, you'll learn what happened to Native Americans on the plains after whites began to arrive.

Disease on the Great Plains

A person who has smallpox

Take a look at this photo. It shows the skin of someone who has a disease called smallpox.

Nobody gets smallpox any more, but in Lewis and Clark's time, people were terrified of the disease because it spread quickly and the people who caught it usually died.

How did the disease get to the Great Plains? Traders from Europe brought smallpox and other diseases. These diseases killed many Native Americans before Lewis and Clark made their journey.

Just before Lewis and Clark's journey, smallpox swept through the villages on the Great Plains. The disease killed about half the Mandan people and thousands from the Arikara tribe. A tribe called the Omaha lost 400 people. Remember the village that had been destroyed by fire? The villagers may have burned it down to try to keep the disease from spreading.

About 30 years after Lewis and Clark's journey, there was another outbreak of smallpox. When it was over, there were only 138 Mandans left. The Mandan way of life was gone forever.

Smallpox hit agricultural people like the Mandans much harder than nomadic tribes like the Teton Sioux. In a village, it was easy for the disease to spread, and it quickly wiped out many people. But the nomadic tribes lived in small groups and moved around a lot, so even if somebody in one group got the disease, the rest of the tribe might still escape it.

A Mandan village

A Sioux village

So as the smallpox epidemic made the Mandans weaker, it helped to make the Teton Sioux the most powerful tribe on the Great Plains. But they wouldn't be powerful for very long.

White Settlers on the Plains

Lewis and Clark's journey showed that it was possible for Americans to live in the West, so, in the 1800s, more and more whites began moving out onto the plains. The white settlers and traders brought trouble to the lives of the Teton Sioux and other Native American tribes.

One of the worst problems was that the great herds of buffalo disappeared from the plains. As settlers built homes and towns, the buffalo had less land to roam around on, and this made it harder for the buffalo to survive.

Also, settlers and army soldiers shot millions of buffalo. They did this to make money from the hides and to make more room on the prairie. At the time of Lewis and Clark's journey, there were 50 million buffalo on the plains, but just 80 years later, there were only 350 left.

There were very few buffalo left after white settlers came to the West.

When the great herds of buffalo were gone, the Sioux had no buffalo meat for food and no hides for shelter, so they became weaker and weaker. The same thing happened to other tribes on the plains.

51

The Sioux tried to fight for their land, but the settlers and the U.S. Army were too strong. The Sioux didn't have enough men or guns to beat them. By the end of the 1800s, the U.S. government forced the Sioux and other Native Americans to move onto small areas of land called **reservations**.

Summary

In this article, you learned how the lives of Native Americans on the Great Plains changed after whites began to arrive. First traders from Europe brought deadly diseases like smallpox to the plains. Later, white settlers began killing the buffalo. Tribes like the Teton Sioux lost the way of life that Lewis and Clark had written about on their journey. Finally, Native Americans were forced to live on reservations and they could no longer move freely in the great West that had been their home.

Glossary

Word	Definition	Page
agricultural	Agricultural tribes were tribes that farmed the land to grow food. They did not move from place to place.	33
blubber	whale fat	26
bull boat	a round boat that was made out of buffalo skin and branches	43
hide	the skin of a large animal like a buffalo or a cow	40
lodge	a kind of Native American house that was made out of wooden posts and dirt	33
nomadic	Nomadic people are people who move from place to place.	31
pemmican	a Native American food made out of meat, berries, and fat	24
reservations	small areas of land where Native Americans were sent by the U.S. government Native Americans were forced to leave their lands and live on reservations.	52

Word	Definition	Page
tan	to treat a buffalo **hide** so that it will last for a long time	41
territory	area	31
tipi	a kind of Native American house that was made with buffalo skin and wooden poles	32

About the Author

Helen Sillett was born in England and lived in the Netherlands and Canada before moving to California as a teenager. She has taught history and literature classes to college students, and reading and writing classes to young adults. She is a writer and editor and has been a member of the Start-to-Finish team for several years.

Helen has loved animals and the outdoors since she was a child. She spends many hours chasing after her dog, Ella, on the hiking trails near their home in Los Angeles.

About the Narrator

Levin O'Connor was born in Geyser, Montana, and moved to Chicago after graduating from Kenyon College in 2001. When he arrived in Chicago, Levin immediately began studying improv. (Improv is a kind of theater where actors create a new play each night in front of the audience.) Levin trained at Second City and Improv Olympic Theater, and now he performs at both the Improv Olympic Theater and the Playground Theater in Chicago.

A Note to the Teacher

Start-to-Finish Core Content books are designed to help students achieve success in reading to learn. From the provocative cover question to the carefully structured and considerate text, these books promote inquiry, active engagement, and understanding. Not only do students learn curriculum-relevant content, but they learn how to read with understanding. Here are some of the features that make these books such powerful aids in teaching and learning.

Structure That Supports Inquiry and Understanding

Core Content books are carefully structured to encourage students to ask questions, identify main ideas, and understand how ideas relate to one another. The structural features of the Gold Core Content books include the following:

- **"Getting Started"**: A concise introduction engages students in the book's topic and explicitly states what they will learn.
- **Clearly focused articles:** Each of the following articles focuses on a single topic at a length that makes for a comfortable session of reading.
- **"Questions This Article Will Answer"**: Provocative questions following the article title reflect the article's main ideas. Each question corresponds to a heading within the article.
- **Article introduction:** An engaging opening leads to a clear statement of the article topic.
- **Carefully worded headings:** The headings within each article are carefully worded to signal the main idea of the section and reflect the opening questions.
- **Clear topic statements:** Within each article section, the main idea is explicitly stated so that students can distinguish it from supporting details.
- **"Summary"**: A brief Summary in each article recaptures the main ideas signaled by the opening questions, text headings, and topic statements.

Text That Is Written for Success™

Every page of a Core Content book is the product of a skilled team of educators, writers, and editors who understand your students' needs. The text features of these books include the following:

- **Mature treatment of grade level curriculum:** Core Content is age and grade-appropriate for the older student who is actively acquiring reading skills. The books also contain information that may be new to any student in the class, empowering Core Content readers to contribute interesting information to class discussions.
- **Idioms and vocabulary:** The text limits the density of new vocabulary and carefully introduces new words, new meanings of familiar words, and idioms. New subject-specific terms are bold-faced and included in the Glossary.
- **Background knowledge:** The text assumes little prior knowledge and anchors the reader using familiar examples and analogies.
- **Sentence structure:** The text uses simple sentence structures whenever possible, but where complex sentences are needed to clarify links between ideas, the structures used are those which research has shown to enhance comprehension.

For More Information

To find out more about Start-to-Finish Core Content, visit www.donjohnston.com for full product information, standards and research base.